THIS MOST AMAZING DAY

compiled by
CHRISTOPHER HERBERT

CHURCH HOUSE PUBLISHING
Church House, Dean's Yard, London SW1P 3NZ

ISBN 0 7151 0431 4

Published 1986 for the General Synod Board of Education
by Church House Publishing

About the Author

The Rev. Christopher Herbert has been Vicar of St Thomas on the Bourne, Farnham, Surrey, since 1981. Before that he was first diocesan Adviser in Children's Work and then Director of Religious Education for the diocese of Hereford. His previous publications include *A Place to Dream* (with John Hencher) for CIO Publishing; *St Paul's, a Place to Dream* (with John Hencher) for the Friends of St Paul's Cathedral; *The Edge of Wonder* (CIO Publishing) and *Be Thou My Vision*, a diary of prayer (Collins).

Contents

Foreword

A new book on prayer by Christopher Herbert is always an event. His sympathy with and understanding for the beginner, his depth of theological insight, his range of reading can probably (though not easily) be paralleled elsewhere, but what is unique to Chris is his ability to make connections: to pull out the implications of a Bible passage and make them clear by matching the passage against some quite unexpected piece of prose or poem. Who else, for example, would link the description of Jesus' appearance to the disciples (John 20. 19–23) with Richard Hughes' account of an earth tremor on a Caribbean island from *High Wind in Jamaica*? And yet, when you read it, how inevitable, how apt, how illuminating.

This book is full of such moments of illumination. Intended for adults, it explores both grief and glory, death and resurrection as it moves from the events of Maundy Thursday through to Easter Day. Designed for private prayer and meditation, the Bible readings – which both tell and expound the Easter story – are each complemented by one or more passages to think about and pray through. It is a book not only for personal devotion, however; clergy will find much here to enrich corporate worship during Holy Week.

All the year round, moreover, *This Most Amazing Day* is a book for the bereaved; not afraid to share the darkness, but always looking in faith towards the light.

Pamela Egan
Publications Officer, General Synod Board of Education

Maundy Thursday

They were now approaching Jerusalem, and when they reached Bethphage and Bethany, at the Mount of Olives, he sent two of his disciples with these instructions: 'Go to the village opposite, and, just as you enter, you will find tethered there a colt which no one has yet ridden. Untie it and bring it here. If anyone asks, "Why are you doing that?", say, "Our Master needs it, and will send it back here without dalay".' So they went off, and found the colt tethered at a door outside in the street. They were untying it when some of the bystanders asked, 'What are you doing, untying that colt?' They answered as Jesus had told them, and were then allowed to take it.

So they brought the colt to Jesus and spread their cloaks on it, and he mounted. And people carpeted the road with their cloaks, while others spread brushwood which they had cut in the fields; and those who went ahead and the others who came behind shouted, 'Hosanna! Blessings on him who comes in the name of the Lord! Blessings on the coming kingdom of our father David! Hosanna in the heavens!'

Mark 11. 1–10

You are a clown or you are not a clown. You are born a clown. The make-up you put on is not a disguise. It is through the make-up that you become yourself.

Annie Fratellini

Maundy Thursday

Jesus was at Bethany in the house of Simon the leper, when a woman came to him with a small bottle of fragrant oil, very costly; and as he sat at the table she began to pour it over his head. The disciples were indignant when they saw it. 'Why this waste?' they said; 'it could have been sold for a good sum and the money given to the poor.' Jesus was aware of this, and said to them, 'Why must you make trouble for the woman? It is a fine thing she has done for me. You have the poor among you always; but you will not always have me. When she poured this oil on my body it was her way of preparing me for burial. I tell you this: wherever in all the world this gospel is proclaimed, what she has done will be told as her memorial.'

Matthew 26. 6–13

The true priest is anybody who is the channel to others of God's love and is willing to share something of the cost of that love; and whose eyes are open to perceive God's presence everywhere and in everybody . . . it has nothing to do with entering a special divinely ordained caste.

H. A. Williams

Maundy Thursday

On the first day of Unleavened Bread the disciples came to ask Jesus, 'Where would you like us to prepare for your Passover supper?' He answered, 'Go to a certain man in the city, and tell him, "The Master says, 'My appointed time is near; I am to keep Passover with my disciples at your house' ".' The disciples did as Jesus directed them and prepared for Passover.

Matthew 26. 17–19

It seems that enquiry and commitment must go forward together hand in hand; continuously side by side. It is a very difficult task to keep them more or less level, but I can't see any other way to make honest progress.

Philip Toynbee

Maundy Thursday

In the evening he sat down with the twelve disciples; and during supper he said, 'I tell you this: one of you will betray me'. In great distress they exclaimed one after the other, 'Can you mean me, Lord?' He answered, 'One who has dipped his hand into this bowl with me will betray me. The Son of Man is going the way appointed for him in the scriptures; but alas for that man by whom the Son of Man is betrayed! It would be better for that man if he had never been born.' Then Judas spoke, the one who was to betray him: 'Rabbi, can you mean me?' Jesus replied, 'The words are yours.'

Matthew 26. 20–25

He had reached the point when the human being realises that no amount of knowing diminishes the amount of the unknown.

Laurens van der Post

Maundy Thursday

During supper Jesus took bread, and having said the blessing he broke it and gave it to the disciples with the words: 'Take this and eat; this is my body.' Then he took a cup, and having offered thanks to God he gave it to them with the words: 'Drink from it, all of you. For this is my blood, the blood of the covenant, shed for many for the forgiveness of sins. I tell you, never again shall I drink from the fruit of the vine until that day when I drink it new with you in the kingdom of my Father.'

Matthew 26. 26–29

Love bade me welcome, yet my soul drew back,
    Guilty of dust and sin.
But quick-eyed Love, observing me grow slack
    From my first entrance in,
Drew nearer to me, sweetly questioning
    If I lacked any thing.

'A guest', I answered, 'worthy to be here.'
    Love said, 'You shall be he.'
'I, the unkind, the ungrateful? Ah, my dear,
    I cannot look on thee.'
Love took my hand, and smiling did reply,
    'Who made the eyes but I?'

'Truth, Lord, but I have marred them; let my shame
    Go where it doth deserve.'
'And know you not', says Love, 'who bore the blame?'
    'My dear, then I will serve.'
'You must sit down,' says Love, 'and taste my meat.'
    So I did sit and eat.

George Herbert

By the grace of God
you have been called to a life
in which everything is inspired
by the sacrament of the Eucharist.
You must grow in daily knowledge
of this mystery,
and in a greater love for the Lord
who gives himself in it.

The celebration of the Eucharist
is the centre of your life.
It is the highest expression
and the strongest support
of your life in community.
It is the beginning and end of your actions;
the source and consummation
of your service to God.

When you celebrate the memorial of Christ
give thanks to God
for his countless benefits.
Never tire of praising him
one in heart and voice with your brothers,
and united with Christ, the sacrifice of praise.
Renew yourself in the spirit of love and unity
because you are sharing with your brothers
the same bread, the same cup.

The celebration of the Eucharist
would be nothing but a romantic or aesthetic sensation
should you forget
that the heart of it
is the self-giving of Jesus.
The sacrifice of yourself for the sake of the others
is the single foundation of every community.
Unite yourself with the Lord, then,
in a fruitful and acceptable offering
for the life of the world.

Rule for a New Brother

Maundy Thursday

Simon Peter said to him, 'Lord, where are you going?' Jesus replied, 'Where I am going you cannot follow me now, but one day you will.' Peter said, 'Lord, why cannot I follow you now? I will lay down my life for you.' Jesus answered, 'Will you indeed lay down your life for me? I tell you in very truth, before the cock crows you will have denied me three times.'

John 13. 36–38

'THIS IS MY BODY' (Mark 14. 12–26)
I am standing in a circle, Lord, among a few of your
    disciples in a small room.
I take a small piece of bread, a sip of wine.
This is your Body and Blood in which we all share.
I look around.
We all have our joys and sorrows, our hopes and
    disappointments.
We will go forth to love as best we can,
    or to face some difficulty with renewed strength,
    or to forget until we meet here again,
    or to deny you with Peter,
    or even perhaps to despair with Judas.
We, Lord, are your Body.
For the short time we meet together,
Draw us closer to yourself,
Make us aware of your presence,
Enable us to remove the sting from those problems that
    arise between us,
Weld us into that type of reconciled community you
    wish mankind to be.
And then 'send us out in the power of your Spirit to live
    and work to your praise and glory'.

Rex Chapman

Maundy Thursday

Oh, I hope I die to the sound of music. Funny if it was all that Radio One stuff that I haven't heard for so long! I never thought I would be nostalgic for some punk and funk, although some real jazz would be nice. Rock and roll? No, I'd rather go back to a bit of Victor Sylvester and get dancing. Perhaps I shall hear 'Sir Roger de Coverley' or 'Strip the Willow'; how lovely to dance over the waters in an eightsome! I'd be quite happy with some Noël Coward, or Edith Piaf . . . and why not Tchaikovsky or something from 'La Traviata'? Or the Hallelujah Chorus.

No, in my heart of hearts I know I long to die to the sound of Russian Orthodox Church music with its booming mystical quality. Or no, why not the 'Misa Criola' from South America, or some African liturgical music? Why not some lovely English church music?

Perhaps Beethoven's ninth symphony . . . no, that wonderful hymn 'Servant of God, remember' . . . and Bach.

Well, it's a catalogue, too much for 'Desert Island Discs', enough for a long journey.

But – WHAT OF THAT MUSIC WE SHALL HEAR?

Anne Shells

Maundy Thursday

(When, through sickness or death or any other circumstance, a person is suddenly removed from his sphere of work and the rhythm of life, and he is helpless to carry out his responsibilities, he is haunted not only with the sense of the unfinished task but by the awful burden he has placed on others.)

Lord, it is Holy Week, when the liturgy of your Church takes us in companionship with you through to Jerusalem and beyond. It is very hard for a priest to be without his people at this time. It is hard to know, as you stay awake through the long nights, of all the unfinished work you have left for others. But in the middle of the night you come, Lord, with your peace. All our work is your work and we place it back into your hands. I do not ask for forgiveness for the unfinished work for you will finish it through your other children whom you have given me as my brothers and sisters, when on the Cross you said 'It is finished'. You included not only your work but my unfinished work as well.

Help me not to be anxious but to rest in you; for always, all through life, you share the load as you have promised and if I cannot continue the journey you are there to finish it. Lord, thank you for the assurance that you give us, thank you for sharing with me in my nights of loneliness in addition to all that you have to bear yourself in redeeming the world. Thank you for letting me share in your cry of victory, 'Alleluia', but Lord, first let me share with you your cry of dereliction from a cross. Don't let me escape, let me be with you, for where you are there is paradise. Let me be with you today, please.

Subir Biswas

Maundy Thursday

(My cook brought his little girl to see me today from his village. This was the first time we had met. Her very shyness and quietness held a beauty that spoke of the shyness of God.)

Forgive us, Lord, when we are so clever, so very sure of ourselves, so bold in speaking out, so ready to give solutions. Help us to be shy, Lord. Today two of the servants brought gifts, a chicken and prawns. They were expensive gifts but given quietly, left in the kitchen. Help me this day to give myself to you in the same quietness and hiddenness as you give yourself to me in the shyness and hiddenness of bread and wine.

Subir Biswas

UNDER A DARK CLOUD

There have been times, O Lord, when I have walked the hill tops with you, when I have felt you near, and my heart has been warm in the remembrance of blessings in the past. But now . . . my heart is dry and cold, moods of depression come over me, prayer seems unreal. You seem hidden, dark clouds descend upon my spirits . . . let me hear you whisper, 'Keep steady, if you cannot give warmth of feeling, give your desire for me, your hunger for me, your emptiness . . . above the dark cloud, my sun is shining always . . . let quick darts of faith pierce the cloud . . . stretch out your hand in the dark . . . you will find my hand near . . . my child, my dear child!'

George Appleton

Maundy Thursday

O Lord Jesus Christ, look upon us with those eyes of yours, the eyes with which you looked upon Peter in the hall of judgement, that with Peter we may repent, and by your great love be forgiven and restored; for your mercy's sake.

Prayers for use at alternative services

Lord Jesus Christ, who when about to institute your holy Sacrament at the Last Supper washed the feet of the apostles, and taught us by your example the grace of humility; cleanse us, we pray, from all stain of sin, that we may be prepared to share your holy mysteries; for you are alive and reign with the Father and the Holy Spirit, one God, now and for ever.

Prayers for use at alternative services

Good Friday

DO NOT GO GENTLE INTO THAT GOOD NIGHT

Do not go gentle into that good night,
Old age should burn and rave at close of day;
Rage, rage against the dying of the light.

Though wise men at their end know dark is right,
Because their words had forked no lightning they
Do not go gentle into that good night.

Good men, the last wave by, crying how bright
Their frail deeds might have danced in a green bay,
Rage, rage against the dying of the light.

Wild men who caught and sang the sun in flight,
And learn, too late, they grieved it on its way,
Do not go gentle into that good night.

Grave men, near death, who see with blinding sight
Blind eyes could blaze like meteors and be gay,
Rage, rage against the dying of the light.

And you, my father, there on the sad height,
Curse, bless, me now with your fierce tears, I pray.
Do not go gentle into that good night.
Rage, rage against the dying of the light.

Dylan Thomas

Good Friday

While he was speaking, Judas, one of the Twelve, appeared; with him was a great crowd armed with swords and cudgels, sent by the chief priests and the elders of the nation. The traitor gave them this sign: 'The one I kiss is your man; seize him'; and stepping forward at once, he said, 'Hail, Rabbi!' and kissed him. Jesus replied, 'Friend, do what you are here to do.' They then came forward, seized Jesus, and held him fast.

At that moment one of those with Jesus reached for his sword and drew it, and he struck at the High Priest's servant and cut off his ear.

Matthew 26. 47–51

Good Friday

But Jesus said to him, 'Put up your sword. All who take the sword die by the sword. Do you suppose that I cannot appeal to my Father, who would at once send to my aid more than twelve legions of angels? But how then could the scriptures be fulfilled, which say that this must be?'

At the same time Jesus spoke to the crowd: 'Do you take me for a bandit, that you have come out with swords and cudgels to arrest me? Day after day I sat teaching in the temple, and you did not lay hands on me. But this has all happened to fulfil what the prophets wrote.'

Then the disciples all deserted him and ran away.

Matthew 26. 52–56

AN EVENING PRAYER

Night approaches now.
For all that has been – thanks.
To all that shall be – yes.

Dag Hammarskjold

Good Friday

Jesus was led off under arrest to the house of Caiaphas the High Priest, where the lawyers and elders were assembled. Peter followed him at a distance till he came to the High Priest's courtyard, and going in he sat down there among the attendants, meaning to see the end of it all.

The chief priests and the whole Council tried to find some allegation against Jesus on which a death-sentence could be based; but they failed to find one, though many came forward with false evidence. Finally two men alleged that he had said, 'I can pull down the temple of God, and rebuild it in three days.' At this the High Priest rose and said to him, 'Have you no answer to the charge that these witnesses bring against you?' But Jesus kept silence. The High Priest then said, 'By the living God I charge you to tell us: Are you the Messiah, the Son of God?' Jesus replied, 'The words are yours. But I tell you this: from now on, you will see the Son of Man seated at the right hand of God and coming on the clouds of heaven.' At these words the High Priest tore his robes and exclaimed, 'Blasphemy! Need we call further witnesses? You have heard the blasphemy. What is your opinion?' 'He is guilty,' they answered; 'he should die.'

Matthew 26. 57–66

The Victorians destroyed Thackeray. It was a needful act of self-defence, for he saw through everything they believed in.

John Carey

Good Friday

Meanwhile Peter was sitting outside in the courtyard when a serving-maid accosted him and said, 'You were there too with Jesus the Galilean.' Peter denied it in face of them all. 'I do not know what you mean', he said. He then went out to the gateway, where another girl, seeing him, said to the people there, 'This fellow was with Jesus of Nazareth.' Once again he denied it, saying with an oath, 'I do not know the man.' Shortly afterwards the bystanders came up and said to Peter, 'Surely you are another of them; your accent gives you away!' At this he broke into curses and declared with an oath: 'I do not know the man.' At that moment a cock crew; and Peter remembered how Jesus had said, 'Before the cock crows you will disown me three times.' He went outside, and wept bitterly.

Matthew 26. 69–75

IN THE MIDST OF LIFE

Death and I are only nodding acquaintances
We have not been formally introduced
But many times I have noticed
The final encounter
Here in this hospice,
I can truly say
That death has been met with dignity.
Who can divine the thoughts
Of a man in close confrontation?
I can only remember
One particular passing
When a man,
With sustained smile,
Pointed out what was for him
Evidently a great light.
Who knows what final revelations
Are received in the last hours?
Lord, grant me a star in the East
As well as a smouldering sunset.

Sidney G. Reeman

Good Friday

Jesus was now brought before the Governor; and as he stood there the Governor asked him, 'Are you the king of the Jews?' 'The words are yours', said Jesus; and to the charges laid against him by the chief priests and elders he made no reply. Then Pilate said to him, 'Do you not hear all this evidence that is brought against you?'; but still he refused to answer one word, to the Governor's great astonishment.

Matthew 27. 11–14

Friday, 16th March or Saturday 17th – lost track of dates, but think the last correct. Tragedy all along the line. At lunch, the day before yesterday, poor Titus Oates said he couldn't go on; he proposed we should leave him in his sleeping-bag. That we could not do, and induced him to come on, on the afternoon march. In spite of its awful nature for him he struggled on and we made a few miles. At night he was worse and we knew the end had come.

Should this be found I want these facts recorded. Oates's last thoughts were of his mother, but immediately before he took pride in thinking that his regiment would be pleased with the bold way in which he met his death. We can testify to his bravery. He has borne intense suffering for weeks without complaint, and to the very last was able and willing to discuss outside subjects. He did not – would not – give up hope to the very end. He was a brave soul. This was the end. He slept through the night before last, hoping not to wake; but he woke in the morning – yesterday. It was blowing a blizzard. He said 'I am just going outside and may be some time'. He went out into the blizzard and we have not seen him since . . .

We knew that poor Oates was walking to his death, but though we tried to dissuade him, we knew it was the act of a brave man and an English gentleman. We all hope to meet the end with a similar spirit, and assuredly the end is not far . . .

Robert Falcon Scott

Good Friday

At the festival season it was the Governor's custom to release one prisoner chosen by the people. There was then in custody a man of some notoriety, called Jesus Bar-Abbas. When they were assembled Pilate said to them, 'Which would you like me to release to you – Jesus Bar-Abbas, or Jesus called Messiah?' For he knew that it was out of malice that they had brought Jesus before him.

While Pilate was sitting in court a message came to him from his wife: 'Have nothing to do with that innocent man; I was much troubled on his account in my dreams last night.'

Meanwhile the chief priests and elders had persuaded the crowd to ask for the release of Bar-Abbas and to have Jesus put to death. So when the Governor asked, 'Which of the two do you wish me to release to you?' they said, 'Bar-Abbas'. 'Then what am I to do with Jesus called Messiah?' asked Pilate; and with one voice they answered, 'Crucify him!' 'Why, what harm has he done?' Pilate asked; but they shouted all the louder, 'Crucify him!'

Pilate could see that nothing was being gained, and a riot was starting; so he took water and washed his hands in full view of the people, saying, 'My hands are clean of this man's blood; see to that yourselves.' And with one voice the people cried, 'His blood be on us, and on our children.' He then released Bar-Abbas to them; but he had Jesus flogged, and handed him over to be crucified.

Matthew 27. 15–26

Good Friday

I rest on God, who will assuredly not allow me to find the meaning of life in his love and forgiveness, to be wholly dependent upon him for the gift of myself, and then destroy that meaning, revoke that gift. He who holds me in existence now, can and will hold me in it still, through and beyond the dissolution of my mortal frame. For this is the essence of love, to affirm the right of the beloved to exist. And what God affirms, nothing and no one can contradict.

John Austin Baker

Good Friday

Pilate's soldiers then took Jesus into the Governor's headquarters, where they collected the whole company round him. They stripped him and dressed him in a scarlet mantle; and plaiting a crown of thorns they placed it on his head, with a cane in his right hand. Falling on their knees before him they jeered at him: 'Hail, King of the Jews!' They spat on him, and used the cane to beat him about the head. When they had finished their mockery, they took off the mantle and dressed him in his own clothes.

Matthew 27. 27–31

PILGRIMAGES

There is an island there is no going
to but in a small boat the way
the saints went, travelling the gallery
of the frightened faces of
the long-drowned, munching the gravel
of its beaches. So I have gone
up the salt lane to the building
with the stone altar and the candles
gone out, and kneeled and lifted
my eyes to the furious gargoyle
of the owl that is like a god
gone small and resentful. There
is no body in the stained window
of the sky now. Am I too late?
Were they too late also, those
first pilgrims? He is such a fast
God, always before us and
leaving as we arrive.

There are those here
not given to prayer, whose office
is the blank sea that they say daily.
What they listen to is not

hymns but the slow chemistry of the soil
that turns saints' bones to dust,
dust to an irritant of the nostril.

There is no time on this island.
The swinging pendulum of the tide
has no clock; the events
are dateless. These people are not
late or soon; they are just
here with only the one question
to ask, which life answers
by being in them. It is I
who ask. Was the pilgrimage
I made to come to my own
self, to learn that in times
like these and for one like me
God will never be plain and
out there, but dark rather and
inexplicable, as though he were in here?

R. S. Thomas

Good Friday

Then they led him away to be crucified. On their way out they met a man from Cyrene, Simon by name, and pressed him into service to carry his cross.

So they came to a place called Golgotha (which means 'Place of a skull') and there he was offered a draught of wine mixed with gall; but when he had tasted it he would not drink.

After fastening him to the cross they divided his clothes among them by casting lots, and then sat down there to keep watch. Over his head was placed the inscription giving the charge: 'This is Jesus the King of the Jews.'

Two bandits were crucified with him, one on his right and the other on his left.

The passers-by hurled abuse at him: they wagged their heads and cried, 'You would pull the temple down, would you, and build it in three days? Come down from the cross and save yourself, if you are indeed the Son of God.' So too the chief priests with the lawyers and elders mocked at him: 'He saved others,' they said, 'but he cannot save himself. King of Israel, indeed! Let him come down now from the cross, and then we will believe him. Did he trust in God? Let God rescue him, if he wants him – for he said he was God's Son.' Even the bandits who were crucified with him taunted him in the same way.

Matthew 27. 32–44

Good Friday

IN MEMORY OF A FELLOW-WORKER

He wasn't alone. His muscles grew into the flesh of the crowd,
energy their pulse, as long as they held a hammer,
as long as his feet felt the ground.
And a stone smashed his temples
and cut through his heart's chamber.

They took his body, and walked in a silent line.

Toil still lingered about him, a sense of wrong.
They wore grey blouses, boots ankle deep in mud.
In this they showed the end.

How violently his time halted: the pointers on the low-voltage dials
jerked, then dropped to zero again.
White stone now within him, eating into his being,
taking over enough of him to turn him into stone.

Who will lift up that stone, unfurl his thoughts again
under the cracked temples? So plaster cracks on the wall.
They laid him down, his back on a sheet of gravel.
His wife came, worn out with worry; his son returned from school.

Should his anger now flow into the anger of others?
It was maturing in him through its own truth and love.
Should he be used by those who come after,
deprived of substance, unique and deeply his own?

The stones on the move again: a wagon bruising the flowers.

Again the electric current cuts deep into the walls.
But the man has taken with him the world's inner structure,
where the greater the anger, the higher the explosion of love.

Karol Wojtyla

From midday a darkness fell over the land, which lasted until three in the afternoon; and about three Jesus cried aloud, 'Eli, Eli, lama sabachthani?', which means, 'My God, my God, why hast thou forsaken me?' Some of the bystanders, on hearing this, said, 'He is calling Elijah'. One of them ran at once and fetched a sponge, which he soaked in sour wine, and held it to his lips on the end of a cane. But the others said, 'Let us see if Elijah will come to save him.'

Jesus again gave a loud cry, and breathed his last.

Matthew 27. 45–50

Good Friday

SUPPOSE

Suppose the stone
Should return again
To the earth
From where it came?

Suppose the glass
And iron should melt
And run away,
Formless once more?

Suppose the music
And all the words
Fell silent
On the still air?

Suppose this church
Should disappear,
Its great design
Become a memory?

Suppose that God
Should love the lost,
And from a ruin
Build a city?

John Hencher

Good Friday

At that moment the curtain of the temple was torn in two from top to bottom.

Matthew 27. 51

THE KILLING

That was the day they killed the Son of God
On a squat hill-top by Jerusalem.
Zion was bare, her children from their maze
Sucked by the demon curiosity
Clean through the gates. The very halt and blind
Had somehow got themselves up to the hill.

After the ceremonial preparation,
The scourging, nailing, nailing against the wood,
Erection of the main-trees with their burden,
While from the hill rose an orchestral wailing,
They were there at last, high up in the soft spring day.
We watched the writhings, heard the moanings, saw
The three heads turning on their separate axles
Like broken wheels left spinning. Round *his* head
Was loosely bound a crown of plaited thorn
That hurt at random, stinging temple and brow
As the pain swung into its envious circle.
In front the wreath was gathered in a knot
That as he gazed looked like the last stump left
Of a death-wounded deer's great antlers. Some
Who came to stare grew silent as they looked,
Indignant or sorry. But the hardened old
And the hard-hearted young, although at odds
From the first morning, cursed him with one curse,
Having prayed for a Rabbi or an armed Messiah
And found the Son of God. What use to them
Was a God or a Son of God? Of what avail
For purposes such as theirs? Beside the cross-foot,
Alone, four women stood and did not move

All day. The sun revolved, the shadow wheeled,
The evening fell. His head lay on his breast,
But in his breast they watched his heart move on
By itself alone, accomplishing its journey.
Their taunts grew louder, sharpened by the knowledge
That he was walking in the park of death,
Far from their rage. Yet all grew stale at last,
Spite, curiosity, envy, hate itself.
They waited only for death and death was slow
And came so quietly they scarce could mark it.
They were angry then with death and death's deceit.
I was a stranger, could not read these people
Or this outlandish deity. Did a God
Indeed in dying cross my life that day
By chance, he on his road and I on mine?

Edwin Muir

Good Friday

And when the centurion and his men who were keeping watch over Jesus saw the earthquake and all that was happening, they were filled with awe, and they said, 'Truly this man was a son of God'.

Matthew 27. 54

Death, be not proud, though some have called thee
Mighty and dreadful; for thou art not so.
For those whom thou think'st thou dost overthrow
Die not, poor Death, nor yet canst thou kill me.
From rest and sleep, which but thy pictures be,
Much pleasure, then from thee much more must flow;
And soonest our best men with thee do go –
Rest of their bones, and soul's delivery.

Thou art slave to Fate, chance, kings and desperate men,
And dost with poison, war, and sickness dwell;
And poppy or charms can make us sleep as well
And better than thy stroke; why swellst thou then?

One short sleep past, we wake eternally
And death shall be no more; Death, thou shalt die.

John Donne

Good Friday

When evening fell, there came a man of Arimathaea, Joseph by name, who was a man of means, and had himself become a disciple of Jesus. He approached Pilate, and asked for the body of Jesus; and Pilate gave orders that he should have it. Joseph took the body, wrapped it in a clean linen sheet, and laid it in his own unused tomb, which he had cut out of the rock; he then rolled a large stone against the entrance, and went away.

Matthew 27. 57–60

God said to Adam: Dust you are, to dust you shall return. This was spoken with the Voice that is Love, and within that dust is the meaning of Love.

Anne Shells

Give rest, O Christ, to thy servant with thy Saints:
where sorrow and pain are no more; neither
sighing, but life everlasting.
Thou only art immortal, the Creator and Maker of man:
and we are mortal, formed of the earth, and unto
earth shall we return:
for so thou didst ordain, when thou createdst me,
saying,
Dust thou art, and unto dust shalt thou return.
All we go down to the dust; and, weeping o'er the grave,
we make our song: alleluya, alleluya, alleluya.

Russian Contakion of the Departed

Good Friday

My earliest recollection of death has one vivid moment: Ssh – hush – tiptoe . . . then I am lifted up to see Dargy, my grandmother, (not to be shown off), and know it is for the last time. It was awesome, she was going to heaven. I was four and knew that my mother was taking care of the whole event, and that it was more important than we were, my brother and I and our new baby sister.

Not till we were holidaying in Switzerland when I was nine was I to meet it memorably again. One night, inexplicably and shockingly, the sound of my mother's sobbing came through the thin wooden walls of the chalet. We had never heard inconsolable sobbing and my father was incapable of calming her. The next day we were told that a cousin, my mother's favourite nephew, had died. But the tragedy of his illness and suicide we were left to find out years later. The mystery of grief was not mentioned, we pretended we had heard nothing and tried to be good all day.

Anne Shells

Good Friday

TEARS

Almighty God, Father of all mankind,
in your Son you took upon yourself
the world's sorrow.
We offer you our own sorrow and sadness
knowing that you can help us to bear our grief
through the infinite understanding and love
of Jesus Christ our Lord.

Christopher Herbert

And, of course, butterflies.
No wonder old people get wrinkled up like cocoons.
Just think what they are going to turn into!

Anne Shells

Good Friday

Grant, O Lord, to all those who are bearing pain, thy spirit of healing, thy spirit of life, thy spirit of peace and hope, of courage and endurance. Cast out from them the spirit of anxiety and fear; grant them perfect confidence and trust in thee, that in thy light they may see light; through Jesus Christ our Lord.

Anon

O Lord our God, who hast reconciled us to thyself and to one another through the death of thy Son, and hast entrusted to us the ministry of reconciliation; keep ever before our hearts and minds the price that thou hast paid for the salvation of the world. Crucify our pride, destroy our enmities; and let the cross of thy Son bear in us all its fruits of righteousness and peace, for his sake.

Suzanne de Dietrich

Blessed Lord, who for our sakes was content to bear sorrow, and want and death, grant unto us such a measure of thy Spirit that we may follow thee in all self-denial and tenderness of soul. Help us by thy great love to succour the afflicted, to relieve the needy and destitute, to share the burdens of the heavy laden, and ever to see thee in all who are poor and desolate, for thine own name's sake.

Bishop Westcott

Good Friday

(On Passion Sunday crosses, made from the wood of shacks of pavement dwellers who were being evicted after twenty years, were blessed and given out to the congregation at St. Paul's Cathedral, as a sign and symbol of the reality of Christ's continuing crucifixion in Calcutta. Cathedral Relief Service after a long battle gained certain rights for them and achieved a rehousing scheme.)

Lord, they were very poor things, just pieces of broken plywood held together with string. Yet, Lord, once upon a time they represented a man's home, his identity, the place from which he set out to work, the place he returned to for love and comfort and rest. It gave him his sense of belonging. It was more than shelter. His dreams were shattered, he was rudely told that he did not belong, he was illegal, he must move but no alternative was given. He was of no consequence, his poverty made that clear. He was a marginal citizen of little value, easily dispensed with.

Lord, you also suffered rejection, you also were marginal to both Church and State, of little consequence; it was expedient that you should be crucified that a nation and city may be saved. Open our eyes, Lord, to see your continued crucifixion in Calcutta. How can we love you if we cannot even see when you suffer in our streets? Forgive our blindness. Forgive us when we are a part of the forces that reject you yet again in this city and crucify you and choose Barabbas.

Subir Biswas

Good Friday

PRAYER OF SAINT PHILIP HOWARD

O Christ, my Lord, which for my sins didst hang upon a tree,
grant that thy grace in me, poor wretch, may still ingrafted be.

Grant that thy naked hanging there may kill in me all pride
and care of wealth, sith thou didst then in such poor state abide.

Grant that thy crown of pricking thorns, which thou for me didst wear,
may make me willing for thy sake all shame and pain to bear.

Grant that those scorns and taunts which thou didst on the cross endure
may humble me, and in my heart all patience still procure.

Grant that thy praying for thy foes may plant within my breast
such charity as from my heart I malice may detest.

Grant that thy pierced hands, which did of nothing all things frame,
may move me to lift up my hand and ever praise thy name.

Grant that thy wounded feet, whose steps were perfect evermore,
may learn my feet to tread those paths which thou hast gone before.

Grant that those drops of blood which ran out from thy heart amain
may meek my heart into salt tears to see thy grievous pain.

Grant that thy blessed grave, wherein thy body lay awhile,
may bury all such vain delights as may my mind defile.

Grant that thy going down to them which did thy sight desire
may keep my soul, when I am dead, clean from the purging fire.

Grant that thy rising up from death may raise my thoughts from sin;
grant that thy parting from this earth from earth my heart may win.

Grant, Lord, that they ascending then may lift my mind to thee
that there my heart and joy may rest, though here in flesh I be. Amen.

St. Philip Howard

Good Friday

O Lover of souls, grant me your eternal love, as I stand by the bedside of the dying. Without your love, I am at the best only doing my duty. Speak through my words and through my silence, through your delegated Love, a word of comfort, trust and expectant hope and joy.
O home of every heart.

George Appleton

O Lord
Remember not only the men and women of goodwill
but also those of ill will.
Do not only remember the suffering they have
inflicted on us, remember the fruits we bought,
thanks to this suffering: our comradeship, our
loyalty, our humility, the courage, the
generosity, the greatness of heart which has
grown out of all this.
And when they come to judgement,
let all the fruits we have borne be their forgiveness.

George Appleton

Lord, all these years we were so close to one another, we did everything together, we seemed to know what each was feeling, without the need of words, and now she is gone. Every memory hurts . . . sometimes there comes the feeling that she is near, just out of sight. Sometimes I feel your reproach that to be so submerged in grief is not to notice that she is as eager to keep in touch with me, as I with her. O dear Lord, I pray out of a sore heart that it may be so, daring to believe that it can be so.

George Appleton

Holy Saturday

No one ever told me that grief felt so like fear. I am not afraid, but the sensation is like being afraid. The same fluttering in the stomach, the same restlessness, the yawning. I keep on swallowing.

At other times it feels like being mildly drunk, or concussed. There is a sort of invisible blanket between the world and me. I find it hard to take in what anyone says. Or perhaps, hard to want to take it in. It is so uninteresting. Yet I want the others to be about me. I dread the moments when the house is empty. If only they would talk to one another and not to me.

There are moments, most unexpectedly, when something inside me tries to assure me that I don't really mind so much, not so very much, after all. Love is not the whole of a man's life. I was happy before I ever met H. I've plenty of what are called 'resources'. People get over these things. Come, I shan't do so badly. One is ashamed to listen to this voice but it seems for a little to be making out a good case. Then comes a sudden jab of red-hot memory and all this 'commonsense' vanishes like an ant in the mouth of a furnace.

On the rebound one passes into tears and pathos. Maudlin tears. I almost prefer the moments of agony. These are at least clean and honest. But the bath of self-pity, the wallow, the loathsome sticky-sweet pleasure of indulging it – that disgusts me. And even while I'm doing it I know it leads me to misrepresent H. herself. Give that mood its head and in a few minutes I shall have substituted for the real woman a mere doll to be blubbered over. Thank God the memory of her is still too strong (will it always be too strong?) to let me get away with it.

For H. wasn't like that at all. Her mind was lithe and quick and muscular as a leopard. Passion, tenderness and pain were all equally unable to disarm it. It scented the first whiff of cant or slush; then sprang, and knocked you over before you knew what was happening. How many bubbles of mine she pricked! I soon learned not to talk rot to her unless I did it for the sheer pleasure – and there's another red-hot jab – of being exposed and laughed at. I was never less silly than as H's lover.

And no one ever told me about the laziness of grief. Except at my job – where the machine seems to run on much as usual – I loathe the slightest effort. Not only writing but even reading a letter is too much. Even shaving. What does it matter now whether my cheek is rough or smooth? They say an unhappy man wants distractions – something to take him out of himself. Only as a dog-tired man wants an extra blanket on a cold night; he'd rather lie there shivering than get up and find one. It's easy to see why the lonely become untidy; finally, dirty and disgusting.

Meanwhile, where is God? This is one of the most disquieting symptoms. When you are happy, so happy that you have no sense of needing him, so happy that you are tempted to feel his claims upon you as in interruption, if you remember yourself and turn to him with gratitude and praise, you will be – or so it feels – welcomed with open arms. But go to him when your need is desperate, when all other help is vain, and what do you find? A door slammed in your face, and a sound of bolting and double bolting on the inside. After that, silence. You may as well turn away. The longer you wait, the more emphatic the silence will become. There are no lights in the windows. It might be an empty house. Was it ever inhabited? It seemed so once. And that seeming was as strong as this. What can this mean? Why is he so present a commander in our time of prosperity and so very absent a help in time of trouble?

C. S. Lewis

Holy Saturday

The crowd who had assembled for the spectacle, when they saw what had happened, went home beating their breasts.

His friends had all been standing at a distance; the women who had accompanied him from Galilee stood with them and watched it all.

Luke 23. 48–49

THE LATE WASP

You that through all the dying summer
Came every morning to our breakfast table,
A lonely bachelor mummer,
And fed on the marmalade
So deeply, all your strength was scarcely able
To prise you from the sweet pit you had made, –
You and the earth have now grown older,
And your blue thoroughfares have felt a change;
They have grown colder;
And it is strange
How the familiar avenues of the air
Crumble now, crumble; the good air will not hold,
All cracked and perished with the cold;
And down you dive through nothing
and through despair.

Edwin Muir

Holy Saturday

The women who had accompanied him from Galilee followed; they took note of the tomb and observed how his body was laid. Then they went home and prepared spices and perfumes; and on the Sabbath they rested in obedience to the commandment.

Luke 23. 55–56

It is all grace. It is not even that there is a door which Christ has unbolted, and we, standing outside it, have to stretch out our hand, lift the latch, and walk through. We are already inside. When our Saviour became man and undid the sin of Adam, he did not command the cherubim with the flaming sword to return to heaven so that we could re-enter Eden. He picked up the walls of Eden and carried them to the farthest edge of Ocean, and there set them up so that they now girdle the whole world. All we are asked to do is to open our eyes and recognise where we are. Once we have done that, then we shall look down at ourselves and our filthy bodies and our tattered clothes, and we shall say, 'I am not fit to be here, in Paradise'; and we shall ask for baptism to wash us clean, and for the white robe of chrism to clothe us in the righteousness of the Lord. But not in order that we may be saved – simply because this is fitting for those who have been saved.

John Austin Baker

Holy Saturday

As soon as she heard that Jesus was on his way, Martha went to meet him, while Mary stayed at home.

Martha said to Jesus, 'If you had been here, sir, my brother would not have died. Even now I know that whatever you ask of God, God will grant you.' Jesus said, 'Your brother will rise again'. 'I know that he will rise again', said Martha, 'at the resurrection on the last day.' Jesus said, 'I am the resurrection and I am life. If a man has faith in me, even though he die, he shall come to life; and no one who is alive and has faith shall ever die. Do you believe this?' 'Lord, I do,' she answered; 'I now believe that you are the Messiah, the Son of God who was to come into the world.'

John 11. 20–27

Holy Saturday

'AFTER MY FUNERAL, GET RID OF MY ASHES.'

Get rid of my ashes,
bury them in a fog, a bog.
The season of my life is over,
I was a breath of God
blown into a lump of clay
before my mother's day.

I lived – and now I'm dead,
burn me, bury my ashes
beneath the sodden heap of leaves
where the blackbirds sport.
I was nothing – am nothing
but a possession of love's energy . . .

. . . I've been taken home.

(And that heap will be useful mould
for the parsnip row.)

Bury me on a dull misty day;
I came from a glory hidden by clouds,
the clouds will be pierced.

If my funeral day is clear and bright –
blue skies reflecting the peace to come
for those travelling on –
go to the sea: an outgoing tide will take my ashes
to the ocean's floor,
among those sands where I still belong,
for the breath of God is within the shore.

Bury me without grief.
I was a thief: greedy for spoils
                    full of conceits
                    a cream-pot licker
                    a lazy lout,

but I loved a lot and I'll go on loving
while my ashes become dust.

Throw those ashes over a river's bridge,
thankful as they float away
that nothing is lost for another day.
Bury me in a storm alongside the sawn shavings
of the felled oak, so huge, old it was;
I will lie safely there
while my true self goes elsewhere.

And the rains and the snows that follow
will make mud for the swallow's nest,
I might be the home of a swallow
while I fly without wings to my own home,
your home,
the HOME of us all.

When you've done –
                    over a cup of tea
                    pray for me.
As I shall be in prayer for you.

And remember to feed the cats.

PS   If it helps a lot
                    to have an exact spot,
                    find St Celther's Well
                    over Cornish fields
                    where, in this life, hell
                    and heaven abide so closely
                    side by side.

Anne Shells

Holy Saturday

We commend unto thee, O Lord,
our souls and our bodies,
our minds and our thoughts,
our prayers and our hopes,
our health and our work,
our life and our death;
our parents and brothers and sisters,
our benefactors and friends,
our neighbours, our countrymen,
and all Christian folk
this day and always.

Bishop Launcelot Andrewes

. . . I never allowed myself to think of a future state, but I always believed that the instant of death is the centre and object of my life. I used to think that, for those who live as they should, it is the instant when, for an infinitesimal fraction of time, pure truth, naked, certain and eternal, enters the soul . . .

Simone Weil

Eternal Light, shine into our hearts,
Eternal Goodness, deliver us from evil,
Eternal Power, be our support,
Eternal Wisdom, scatter the darkness of our ignorance,
Eternal Pity, have mercy upon us;
that with all our heart and mind and soul and
strength we may seek thy face and be brought
by thine infinite mercy to thy holy presence;
through Jesus Christ our Lord.

Alcuin (735–804)

Holy Saturday

Abide with us, Lord, for it is toward evening and the day is far spent. Abide with us and with thy whole Church. Abide with us in the end of the day, in the end of our life, in the end of the world. Abide with us with thy grace and bounty, with thy holy word and sacrament, with thy comfort and thy blessing. Abide with us when over us cometh the night of affliction and fear, the night of doubt and temptation, the night of bitter death. Abide with us and with all thy faithful, through time and eternity.

Lohe (1808–1872)

THE TROUBLES OF THE WORLD

We bring before Thee, O Lord,
the troubles and perils of peoples and nations,
the sighing of prisoners and captives,
the sorrows of the bereaved,
the necessities of strangers,
the helplessness of the weak,
the despondency of the weary,
the failing powers of the aged.
O Lord, draw near to each,
for the sake of Jesus Christ our Lord.

St Anselm

Holy Saturday

Save us, O Lord, waking, and guard us sleeping, that awake we may watch with Christ, and asleep we may rest in peace.

The Service of Compline

(A nurse sits up all night watching the monitor of a heart patient. She has two little boys and both have fever and she is worried about them. It is not easy for her to be awake all night, to be patient and kind to her patients who are full of anxiety or sleeplessness or complaints. She has to work twelve hours before she can go home. If you try to sympathise, she only says repeatedly, 'I am only doing my duty.')

Lord, when I sleep in comfort each night and feel that I have earned my rest, help me to remember all those in this city whose work it is to stay awake besides beds of suffering. Forgive me that I take so much for granted. Give me gratitude for these your servants of your kingdom through whom you work anonymously and silently.

Subir Biswas

Holy Saturday

Almighty and eternal God, your only-begotten Son went down into the grave and came up from thence in glory; grant that, through his resurrection, your faithful who have been buried with him in baptism may journey safely to everlasting life, through Christ our Lord. Amen.

Anon

O my God, I have no idea where I am going. I do not see the road ahead of me . . . Nor do I really know myself, and the fact that I think I am following your will does not mean that I am actually doing so. But I desire to do your will, and I know the very desire pleases you. Therefore I will trust you always though I may seem to be lost. I will not fear, for you are always with me, O my dear God.

Thomas Merton

Easter Day

Early on the Sunday morning, while it was still dark, Mary of Magdala came to the tomb. She saw that the stone had been moved away from the entrance, and ran to Simon Peter and the other disciple, the one whom Jesus loved. 'They have taken the Lord out of his tomb', she cried, 'and we do not know where they have laid him.' So Peter and the other set out and made their way to the tomb. They were running side by side, but the other disciple outran Peter and reached the tomb first. He peered in and saw the linen wrappings lying there, but did not enter. Then Simon Peter came up, following him, and he went into the tomb. He saw the linen wrappings lying, and the napkin which had been over his head, not lying with the wrappings but rolled together in a place by itself. Then the disciple who had reached the tomb first went in too, and he saw and believed; until then they had not understood the scriptures, which showed that he must rise from the dead.

So the disciples went home again; but Mary stood at the tomb outside, weeping.

John 20. 1–10

'The trees are singing my music, or am I singing theirs?'

Sir Edward Elgar, on 'The Dream of Gerontius'

Easter Day

(Christian and Hopeful have come through the river of death)

Now upon the bank of the river, on the other side, they saw the two shining men again, who there waited for them. Wherefore being come out of the river, they saluted them, saying, We are ministering spirits, sent forth to minister for those that shall be heirs of salvation. Thus they went along towards the gate.

Now you must note, that the City stood upon a mighty hill; but the pilgrims went up that hill with ease, because they had these two men to lead them up by the arms; also they had left their mortal garments behind them in the river; for though they went in with them, they came out without them. They therefore went up here with much agility and speed, though the foundation upon which the City was framed was higher than the clouds; they therefore went up through the regions of the air, sweetly talking as they went, being comforted because they had safely got over the river, and had such glorious companions to attend them.

The talk that they had with the shining ones was about the glory of the place; who told them that the beauty and glory of it was inexpressible. There, said they, is the Mount Sion, the heavenly Jerusalem, the innumerable company of angels, and the spirits of just men made perfect. You are going now, said they, to the paradise of God, wherein you shall see the tree of life, and eat of the never-fading fruits thereof: and when you come there you shall have white robes given you, and your walk and talk shall be every day with the King, even all the days of eternity. There you shall not see again such things as you saw when you were in the lower region upon the earth: to wit, sorrow, sickness, affliction and death; for the former things are passed away. The men then asked,

What must we do in the holy place? To whom it was answered, You must there receive the comfort of all your toil, and have joy for all your sorrow; you must reap what you have sown, even the fruit of all your prayers, and tears, and sufferings for the King by the way. In that place you must wear crowns of gold, and enjoy the perpetual sight and visions of the Holy One; for there you shall see him as he is. There also you shall serve him continually.

John Bunyan, 'The Pilgrim's Progress'

Easter Day

As she wept, she peered into the tomb; and she saw two angels in white sitting there, one at the head, and one at the feet, where the body of Jesus had lain. They said to her, 'Why are you weeping?' She answered, 'They have taken my Lord away, and I do not know where they have laid him.' With these words she turned round and saw Jesus standing there, but did not recognise him. Jesus said to her, 'Why are you weeping? Who is it you are looking for?' Thinking it was the gardener, she said, 'If it is you, sir, who removed him, tell me where you have laid him, and I will take him away.' Jesus said, 'Mary!' She turned to him and said, 'Rabbuni!' (which is Hebrew for 'My Master'). Jesus said, 'Do not cling to me, for I have not yet ascended to the Father. But go to my brothers, and tell them that I am now ascending to my Father and your Father, my God and your God.' Mary of Magdala went to the disciples with her news: 'I have seen the Lord!' she said, and gave them his message.

John 20. 11–18

Easter Day

David stumbled, staggered, crawled: onwards in the darkness, uphill all the time, the going hard and stony: it must be a mountain slope . . . Then he came to a road and staggered across it without even remembering to see if there were people about . . . then farther uphill where something was growing in low straight lines . . . then over another stretch of mountainside with hard sharp-edged stones that hurt his feet. And then he could go no farther.

But there was no one to disturb his sleep that night, and when he woke he was no longer tired. He was not even cold – he was pleasantly warm, in fact. He lay awake for a while with his eyes shut, basking in the warmth of his own body while he listened as usual for sounds about him. But all was quiet. Then opening his eyes he sat up and looked.

David was familiar only with various tones of grey and brown, and of course the blue of the sky. Well, yes, he had once seen a little red flower that had strayed inside the camp wall. Apart from that, colour was something he had only heard of: he had seen only a pale and muddied reflection of it – in the ugliness of the camp and the equally ugly quarters of the guards.

He did not know how long he stayed there on the mountainside, sitting motionless, just gazing . . . only when everything grew strangely misty did he discover that he was crying.

Far below him lay the sea, a sea bluer than any sky he had ever seen. The land curved in and out along its edge: in and out, up and down, all green and golden, with here and there the red of flowers too far off to be clearly seen. Down by the sea a road ran along the foot of the mountain, and near it lay villages whose bright colours gleamed dazzlingly. There were trees with many changing tints of green, and over it all shone the warming sun – not white-hot and spiteful and scorching, as the sun had shone upon the camp in the summertime, but with a warm golden loveliness.

Beauty. David had once heard Johannes use the word. It must have been something like this he meant . . . perhaps that was why he had come back and gone with him to Salonica, so that he, David, could sail across the sea till he came to a place where things were beautiful.

His tears continued to flow, faster and faster, and he brushed them angrily away so that the mist before his eyes should not veil that beauty from him.

Suddenly he knew that he did not want to die.

Anne Holm, 'I am David'

Easter Day

One of the Twelve, Thomas, that is 'the Twin', was not with the rest when Jesus came. So the disciples told him, 'We have seen the Lord.' He said, 'Unless I see the mark of the nails on his hands, unless I put my finger into the place where the nails were, and my hand into his side, I will not believe it.'

A week later his disciples were again in the room, and Thomas was with them. Although the doors were locked, Jesus came and stood among them, saying, 'Peace be with you!' Then he said to Thomas, 'Reach your finger here; see my hands. Reach your hand here and put it into my side. Be unbelieving no longer, but believe.' Thomas said, 'My Lord and my God!'

John 20. 24–28

I THANK YOU GOD FOR MOST THIS AMAZING

i thank you god for most this amazing
day: for the leaping greenly spirits of trees
and a blue true dream of sky; and for everything
which is natural which is infinite which is yes

(i who have died am alive again today,
and this is the sun's birthday; this is the birth
day of life and of love and wings: and of the gay
great happening illimitably earth)

how should tasting touching hearing seeing
breathing any – lifted from the no
of all nothing – human merely being
doubt unimaginable you?

(now the ears of my ears awake and
now the eyes of my eyes are opened)

e.e. cummings

Easter Day

Late that Sunday evening, when the disciples were together behind locked doors, for fear of the Jews, Jesus came and stood among them. 'Peace be with you!' he said, and then showed them his hands and his side. So when the disciples saw the Lord, they were filled with joy. Jesus repeated, 'Peace be with you!', and said, 'As the Father sent me, so I send you.' Then he breathed on them, saying, 'Receive the Holy Spirit! If you forgive any man's sins, they stand forgiven; if you pronounce them unforgiven, unforgiven they remain.'

John 20. 19–23

An hour or so after noon they clustered together, puffy from the warm water, in the insufficient shade of a Panama fern, ate such of the food they had brought as they had appetite for; and drank all the water, wishing for more. Then a very odd thing happened: for even as they sat there they heard the most peculiar sound: a strange, rushing sound that passed overhead like a gale of wind – but not a breath of breeze stirred, that was the odd thing: followed by a sharp hissing and hurting, like a flight of rockets, or gigantic swans – very distant rocs, perhaps – on the wing. They all looked up: but there was nothing at all. The sky was empty and lucid. Long before they were back in the water again all was still. Except that after a while John noticed a sort of tapping, as if someone were gently knocking the outside of a bath you were in. But the bath they were in had no outside, it was solid world. It was funny.

By sunset they were so weak from long immersion they could barely stand up, and as salted as bacon: but, with some common impulse, just before the sun went down they all left the rocks and went and stood by their clothes, where the ponies were tethered, under some palms. As he sank, the sun grew even larger: and instead of red was now a sodden purple. Down he went, behind the western horn of the bay, which blackened till its water-line disappeared and substance and reflection seemed one sharp symmetrical pattern.

Not a breath of breeze even yet ruffled the water: yet momentarily it trembled of its own accord, shattering the reflections: then was glassy again. On that the children held their breath, waiting for it to happen.

A school of fish, terrified by some purely submarine event thrust their heads right out of the water, squattering across the bay in an arrowy rush, dashing up sparkling ripples with the tiny heave of their shoulders: yet after each disturbance all was soon like hardest, dark, thick glass.

Once things vibrated slightly, like a chair in a concert-room: and again there was that mysterious winging, though there was nothing visible beneath the swollen iridescent stars.

Then it came. The water of the bay began to ebb away, as if some one had pulled up the plug: a foot or so of sand and coral gleamed for a moment new to the air: then back the sea rushed in miniature rollers which splashed right up to the feet of the palms. Mouthfuls of turf were torn away: and on the far side of the bay a small piece of cliff tumbled into the water: sand and twigs showered down, dew fell from the trees like diamonds: birds and beasts, their tongues at last loosed, screamed and bellowed: the ponies, though quite unalarmed, lifted up their heads and yelled.

That was all: a few moments. Then silence, with a rapid counter-march, recovered all his rebellious kingdom. Stillness again. The trees moved as little as the pillars of a ruin, each leaf laid sleekly in place. The bubbling foam subsided: the reflections of the stars came out among it as if from clouds. Silent, still, dark, placid, as if there could never have been a disturbance. The naked children too continued to stand motionless beside the quiet ponies, dew on their hair and eyelashes, shine on their infantile round paunches.

But as for Emily, it was too much. The earthquake went completely to her head. She began to dance, hopping laboriously from one foot to another. John caught the infection. He turned head over heels on the damp sand, over and over in an elliptical course, till before he knew it he was in the water, and so giddy as hardly to be able to tell up from down.

Richard Hughes, 'High Wind in Jamaica'

Easter Day

On that same day two of Jesus' followers were going to a village named Emmaus, about eleven kilometres from Jerusalem, and they were talking to each other about all the things that had happened. As they talked and discussed, Jesus himself drew near and walked along with them; they saw him, but somehow did not recognise him. Jesus said to them, 'What are you talking about to each other, as you walk along?'

They stood still, with sad faces. One of them, named Cleopas, asked him, 'Are you the only visitor in Jerusalem who doesn't know the things that have been happening there these last few days?'

'What things?' he asked.

'The things that happened to Jesus of Nazareth,' they answered. 'This man was a prophet and was considered by God and by all the people to be powerful in everything he said and did. Our chief priests and rulers handed him over to be sentenced to death, and he was crucified.

'And we had hoped that he would be the one who was going to set Israel free! Besides all that, this is now the third day since it happened. Some of the women of our group surprised us; they went at dawn to the tomb, but could not find his body. They came back saying they had seen a vision of angels who told them that he is alive. Some of our group went to the tomb and found it exactly as the women had said, but they did not see him.'

Then Jesus said to them, 'How foolish you are, how slow you are to believe everything the prophets said! Was it not necessary for the Messiah to suffer these things and then to enter his glory?' And Jesus explained to them what was said about himself in all the Scriptures, beginning with the books of Moses and the writings of all the prophets.

As they came near the village to which they were going, Jesus acted as if he were going farther; but they held him back, saying, 'Stay with us; the day is almost over and it is getting dark.' So he went in to stay with them. He sat down to eat with them, took the bread, and said the blessing; then he broke the bread and gave it to them. Then their eyes were opened and they recognised him, but he disappeared from their sight. They said to each other, 'Wasn't it like a fire burning in us when he talked to us on the road and explained the Scriptures to us?'

They got up at once and went back to Jerusalem, where they found the eleven disciples gathered together with the others and saying, 'The Lord is risen indeed! He has appeared to Simon!'

The two then explained to them what had happened on the road, and how they had recognised the Lord when he broke the bread.

Luke 24. 13–35

Easter Day

They all listened.

In the darkness something was happening at last. A voice had begun to sing. It was very far away and Digory found it hard to decide from what direction it was coming. Sometimes it seemed to come from all directions at once. Sometimes he almost thought it was coming out of the earth beneath them. Its lower notes were deep enough to be the voice of the earth herself. There were no words. There was hardly even a tune. But it was, beyond comparison, the most beautiful voice he had ever heard. It was so beautiful he could hardly bear it. The horse seemed to like it too: he gave the sort of whinny a horse would give if, after years of being a cab-horse, it found itself back in the old field where it had played as a foal, and saw someone whom it remembered and loved coming across the field to bring it a lump of sugar.

'Gawd!' said the Cabby. 'Ain't it lovely?'

Then two wonders happened at the same moment. One was that the voice was suddenly joined by other voices, more voices than you could possibly count. They were in harmony with it, but far higher up the scale: cold, tingling, silvery voices. The second wonder was that the blackness overhead, all at once, was blazing with stars. They didn't come out gently one by one, as they do on a summer evening. One moment there had been nothing but darkness; next moment a thousand, thousand points of light leaped out – single stars, constellations, and planets, brighter and bigger than any in our world. There were no clouds. The new stars and the new voices began at exactly the same time. If you had seen and heard it, as Digory did, you would have felt quite certain that it was the stars themselves which were singing, and that it was the First Voice, the deep one, which had made them appear and made them sing.

C. S. Lewis, 'The Magician's Nephew'

Easter Day

I consider that what we suffer at this present time cannot be compared at all with the glory that is going to be revealed to us. All of creation waits with eager longing for God to reveal his sons. For creation was condemned to lose its purpose, not of its own will, but because God willed it to be so. Yet there was the hope that creation itself would one day be set free from its slavery to decay and would share the glorious freedom of the children of God. For we know that up to the present time all of creation groans with pain, like the pain of child-birth. But it is not just creation alone which groans; we who have the Spirit as the first of God's gifts also groan within ourselves, as we wait for God to make us his sons and set our whole being free. For it was by hope that we were saved; but if we see what we hope for, then it is not really hope. For who hopes for something he sees? But if we hope for what we do not see, we wait for it with patience.

In the same way the Spirit also comes to help us, weak as we are. For we do not know how we ought to pray; the Spirit himself pleads with God for us in groans that words cannot express. And God, who sees into our hearts, knows what the thought of the Spirit is; because the Spirit pleads with God on behalf of his people and in accordance with his will.

We know that in all things God works for good with those who love him, those whom he has called according to his purpose. Those whom God had already chosen he also set apart to become like his Son, so that the Son would be the first among many brothers. And so those whom God set apart, he called; and those he called, he put right with himself, and he shared his glory with them.

Romans 8. 18–30

Easter Day

Brother,
you want to seek God with all your life,
and love him with all your heart.

But you would be wrong
if you thought you could reach him.
Your arms are too short, your eyes are too dim,
your heart and understanding too small.

To seek God
means first of all
to let yourself be found by him.
He is the God of Abraham, Isaac and Jacob.
He is the God of Jesus Christ.
He is your God,
not because he is yours
but because you are his.

To choose God
is to realise that you are known and loved
in a way surpassing anything men can imagine,
loved before anyone had thought of you
or spoken your name.

To choose God
means giving yourself up to him in faith.
Let your life be built on this faith
as on an invisible foundation.
Let yourself be carried by this faith
like a child in its mother's womb.

And so,
don't talk too much about God
but live
in the certainty that he has written your name
on the palm of his hand.
Live your human task
in the liberating certainty
that nothing in the world can separate you
from God's love for you.

Rule for a New Brother

Easter Day

In view of all this, what can we say? If God is for us, who can be against us? Certainly not God, who did not even keep back his own Son, but offered him for us all! He gave us his Son – will he not also freely give us all things? Who will accuse God's chosen people? God himself declares them not guilty! Who, then, will condemn them? Not Christ Jesus, who died, or rather, who was raised to life and is at the right-hand side of God, pleading with him for us! Who, then, can separate us from the love of Christ? Can trouble do it, or hardship or persecution or hunger or poverty or danger or death? As the scripture says,

'For your sake we are in danger of
death at all times;
we are treated like sheep that are
going to be slaughtered.'

No, in all these things we have complete victory through him who loved us! For I am certain that nothing can separate us from his love: neither death nor life, neither angels nor other heavenly rulers or powers, neither the present nor the future, neither the world above nor the world below – there is nothing in all creation that will ever be able to separate us from the love of God which is ours through Christ Jesus our Lord.

Romans 8. 31–39

Easter Day

Do you wish to understand your Lord's meaning?
Understand truly: Love was his meaning.
Who revealed it to you? Love.
What did he show you? Love.
Why did he show it? For love.
Hold firmly to this and you will learn and know more of this. But you will never know or learn anything other than this, ever.

Julian of Norwich

Easter Day

When I came to you, my brothers, to preach God's secret truth, I did not use big words and great learning. For while I was with you, I made up my mind to forget everything except Jesus Christ and especially his death on the cross. So when I came to you, I was weak and trembled all over with fear, and my teaching and message were not delivered with convincing proof of the power of God's Spirit. Your faith, then, does not rest on human wisdom but on God's power.

Yet I do proclaim a message of wisdom to those who are spiritually mature. But it is not the wisdom that belongs to this world or to the powers that rule this world – powers that are losing their power. The wisdom I proclaim is God's secret wisdom, which is hidden from mankind, but which he had already chosen for our glory even before the world was made. None of the rulers of this world knew this wisdom. If they had known it, they would not have crucified the Lord of glory. However, as the scripture says,

> 'What no one ever saw or heard,
> what no one ever thought could happen,
> is the very thing God prepared for those who love
> him.'

But it was to us that God made known his secret by means of his Spirit. The Spirit searches everything, even the hidden depths of God's purposes. It is only a person's own spirit within him that knows all about him; in the same way, only God's Spirit knows all about God. We have not received this world's spirit; instead, we have received the Spirit sent by God, so that we may know all that God has given us.

I Corinthians 2. 1–12

Easter Day

And now I want to remind you, my brothers, of the Good News which I preach to you, which you received, and on which your faith stands firm. That is the gospel, the message that I preach to you. You are saved by the gospel if you hold firmly to it – unless it was for nothing that you believed.

I passed on to you what I received, which is of the greatest importance: that Christ died for our sins, as written in the Scriptures; that he was buried and that he was raised to life three days later, as written in the Scriptures; that he appeared to Peter and then to all twelve apostles. Then he appeared to more than five hundred of his followers at once, most of whom are still alive, although some have died. Then he appeared to James, and afterwards to all the apostles.

Last of all he appeared also to me – even though I am like someone whose birth was abnormal. For I am the least to be called an apostle, because I persecuted God's church. But by God's grace I am what I am, and the grace that he gave me was not without effect. On the contrary, I have worked harder than any of the other apostles, although it was not really my own doing, but God's grace working with me. So then, whether it came from me or from them, this is what we all preach, and this is what you believe.

I Corinthians 15. 1–11

Easter Day

One chilly, blustery morning in March, I cannot tell exactly how many springs later, Hazel was dozing and waking in his burrow. He had spent a good deal of time there lately, for he felt the cold and could not seem to smell or run so well as in days gone by. He had been dreaming in a confused way – something about rain and elder bloom – when he woke to realise that there was a rabbit lying quietly beside him – no doubt some young buck who had come to ask his advice. The sentry in the run outside should not really have let him in without asking first. Never mind, thought Hazel. He raised his head and said, 'Do you want to talk to me?'

'Yes, that's what I've come for,' replied the other. 'You know me, don't you?'

'Yes, of course,' said Hazel, hoping he would be able to remember his name in a moment. Then he saw that in the darkness of the burrow, the stranger's ears were shining with a faint, silver light. 'Yes, my Lord,' he said. 'Yes, I know you.'

'You've been feeling tired,' said the stranger, 'but I can do something about that. I've come to ask whether you'd care to join my Owsla. We shall be glad to have you and you'll enjoy it. If you're ready, we might go along now.'

They went out past the young sentry, who paid the visitor no attention. The sun was shining and in spite of the cold there were a few bucks and does at silflay, keeping out of the wind as they nibbled the shoots of spring grass. It seemed to Hazel that he would not be needing his body any more, so he left it lying on the edge of the ditch, but stopped for a moment to watch his rabbits and to try to get used to the extraordinary feeling that strength and speed were flowing inexhaustibly out of him into their sleek young bodies and healthy senses.

‘You needn’t worry about them,’ said his companion. ‘They’ll be all right – and thousands like them. If you’ll come along, I’ll show you what I mean.’

He reached the top of the bank in a single, powerful leap. Hazel followed; and together they slipped away, running easily down through the wood, where the first primroses were beginning to bloom.

Richard Adams, ‘Watership Down’

Easter Day

Now, since our message is that Christ has been raised from death, how can some of you say that the dead will not be raised to life? If that is true, it means that Christ was not raised; and if Christ has not been raised from death, then we have nothing to preach and you have nothing to believe. More than that, we are shown to be lying about God, because we said that he raised Christ from death – but if it is true that the dead are not raised to life, then he did not raise Christ. For if the dead are not raised, neither has Christ been raised. And if Christ has not been raised, then your faith is a delusion and you are still lost in your sins. It would also mean that the believers in Christ who have died are lost. If our hope in Christ is good for this life only and no more, then we deserve more pity than anyone else in all the world.

But the truth is that Christ has been raised from death, as the guarantee that those who sleep in death will also be raised. For just as death came by means of a man, in the same way the rising from death comes by means of a man. For just as all people die because of their union with Adam, in the same way all will be raised to life because of their union with Christ.

I Corinthians 15. 12–22

Easter Day

THE VOYAGE BACK

It was the time of voyaging back. It was the time, now at last.
We had come to the end of the days and nights we went patrolling
The wastes of ocean. We'll not retrace our wake, all that is past;
The salt-bleached struggling ship, the frozen spray in the rigging,
Like filigree icing, and the sight of seamen's wind-scored faces
As they hump the shells, with blue-red hands, to the taut whitened,
Intractable single-whip tackle while the ship plunges and races,
Shudders and slips to the slash of the waves, and the stomach feels tightened
In a gritted, queasy contraction, and the smell from the galley
Swims in the head, and the staler stench of tobacco smoke stains
Fingers and mouth. To watch no more for the green break of light that stilly
Creeps out of the spume to etch again the twisted convoy lanes,
And later the stretched off stragglers hove up from the pallid mouth
Of a snowing dawn. To feel, to know, to touch this no more,
To say it is done, for a few years at least, makes the heart want to shout
With the joy of relief for the flesh that was flayed by the raw
Wracking winds from the south and the west. Praise God, it was the last, last time;
We were just about at the end of the rope, waking or sleeping,

We dreamed of the plunge and the rise and the endless wind and the rime.
Of the needling frost that ate its way into eyes and ears and brain.
No wonder I saw a young seaman his face puckered and weeping
As we ran in the lee of the land back to port and he felt the rain
Falling quietly down from a sky that stood still, out of a peace
That spelled home, gentleness, love. His tears were only the tears of release.

R. C. M. Howard

Easter Day

Listen to this secret truth: we shall not all die, but when the last trumpet sounds, we shall all be changed in an instant, as quickly as the blinking of an eye. For when the trumpet sounds, the dead will be raised, never to die again, and we shall all be changed. For what is mortal must be changed into what is immortal; what will die must be changed into what cannot die. So when this takes place, and the mortal has been changed into the immortal, then the scripture will come true: 'Death is destroyed; victory is complete!'

'Where, Death, is your victory?
Where, Death, is your power to hurt?'

Death gets its power to hurt from sin, and sin gets its power from the Law. But thanks be to God who gives us the victory through our Lord Jesus Christ!

I Corinthians 15. 51–57

Easter Day

EASTER WINGS

Lord, who created man in wealth and store,
Though foolishly he lost the same,
decaying more and more,
till he became
most poor,

with thee
Oh let me rise,
as larks, harmoniously,
and sing this day thy victory:
then shall that fall further the flight in me.

My tender age in sorrow did begin,
and still with sickness and shame
thou didst so punish sin
that I became
most thin.

With thee
let me combine,
and feel this day thy victory:
for if I graft my wing on thine,
affliction shall advance the flight in me.

George Herbert

Easter Day

God in his mercy has given us this work to do, and so we are not discouraged. We put aside all secret and shameful deeds: we do not act with deceit, nor do we falsify the word of God. In the full light of truth we live in God's sight and try to commend ourselves to everyone's good conscience. For if the gospel we preach is hidden, it is hidden only from those who are being lost. They do not believe, because their minds have been kept in the dark by the evil god of this world. He keeps them from seeing the light shining on them, the light that comes from the Good News about the glory of Christ, who is the exact likeness of God. For it is not ourselves that we preach; we preach Jesus Christ as Lord, and ourselves as your servants for Jesus' sake. The God who said, 'Out of darkness the light shall shine!' is the same God who made his light shine in our hearts, to bring us the knowledge of God's glory shining in the face of Christ.

II Corinthians 4. 1–6

Easter Day

We are tempted to believe that, although the Resurrection may be the climax of the Gospel, there is yet a Gospel that stands upon its own feet and may be understood and appreciated before we pass on to the Resurrection. The first disciples did not find it so. For them the Gospel without the Resurrection was not merely a Gospel without its final chapter: it was not a Gospel at all. Jesus Christ had, it is true, taught and done great things: but he did not allow the disciples to rest in these things. He led them on to paradox, perplexity and darkness; and there he left them. There too they would have remained, had he not been raised from death. But his Resurrection threw its own light backwards upon the death and the ministry that went before; it illuminated the paradoxes and disclosed the unity of his words and deeds. As Scott Holland said: 'In the Resurrection it was not only the Lord who was raised from the dead. His life on earth rose with him; it was lifted up into its real light.'

A. M. Ramsey

Easter Day

For this reason I fall on my knees before the Father, from whom every family in heaven and on earth receives its true name. I ask God from the wealth of his glory to give you power through his Spirit to be strong in your inner selves, and I pray that Christ will make his home in your hearts through faith, I pray that you may have your roots and foundation in love, so that you, together with all God's people, may have the power to understand how broad and long, how high and deep, is Christ's love. Yes, may you come to know his love – although it can never be fully known – and so be completely filled with the very nature of God.

To him who by means of his power working in us is able to do so much more than we can ever ask for, or even think of: to God be the glory in the church and in Christ Jesus for all time, for ever and ever! Amen.

Ephesians 3. 14–21

Easter Day

Into that house they shall enter
and in that house they shall dwell
where there shall be
    no cloud nor sun
    no darkness nor dazzling
but one equal light;
    no noise or silence
but one equal music;
    no fears or hopes
but one equal possession;
    no foes nor friends
but one equal eternity.

Keep us, Lord,
so awake in the duties of our callings
that we may thus sleep in thy peace
and wake in thy glory.

John Donne

Easter Day

Finally, build up your strength in union with the Lord and by means of his mighty power. Put on all the armour that God gives you, so that you will be able to stand up against the Devil's evil tricks. For we are not fighting against human beings but against the wicked spiritual forces in the heavenly world, the rulers, authorities, and cosmic powers of this dark age. So put on God's armour now! Then when the evil day comes, you will be able to resist the enemy's attacks: and after fighting to the end, you will still hold your ground.

So stand ready, with truth as a belt right round your waist, with righteousness as your breastplate, and as your shoes the readiness to announce the Good News of peace. At all times carry faith as a shield; for with it you will be able to put out all the burning arrows shot by the Evil One. And accept salvation as a helmet, and the word of God as the sword which the Spirit gives you. Do all this in prayer, asking for God's help. Pray on every occasion, as the Spirit leads. For this reason keep alert and never give up; pray always for all God's people.

Ephesians 6. 10–18

Easter Day

THE MOMENT OF ECSTASY

This life is a period of training, a time of preparation, during which we learn the art of loving God and our neighbour, the heart of the Gospel message, sometimes succeeding, sometimes failing.

Death is the way which leads us to the vision of God, the moment when we shall see Him as He really is, and find our total fulfilment in love's final choice.

The ultimate union with that which is most lovable, union with God, is the moment of ecstasy, the unending 'now' of complete happiness. That vision will draw from us the response of surprise, wonder and joy which will be forever our prayer of praise. We are made for that.

Basil Hume

Easter Day

Your life in Christ makes you strong, and his love comforts you. You have fellowship with the Spirit, and you have kindness and compassion for one another. I urge you, then, to make me completely happy by having the same thoughts, sharing the same love, and being one in soul and mind. Don't do anything from selfish ambition or from a cheap desire to boast, but be humble towards one another, always considering others better than yourselves. And look out for one another's interest, not just for your own. The attitude you should have is the one that Christ Jesus had:

He always had the nature of God
but he did not think that by force
he should try to become equal
with God.
Instead of this, of his own free will he
gave up all he had,
and took the nature of a servant.
He became like man
and appeared in human likeness.
He was humble and walked the path
of obedience all the way to death –
his death on the cross.
For this reason God raised him to the
highest place above
and gave him the name that is greater
than any other name.
And so, in honour of the name of Jesus
all beings in heaven, on earth, and
in the world below
will fall on their knees,
and all will openly proclaim that
Christ is Lord,
to the glory of God the Father.

Philippians 2. 1–11

Easter Day

THE WINDHOVER

I caught this morning morning's minion, king-
    dom of daylight's dauphin, dapple-dawn-drawn
        Falcon, in his riding
    Of the rolling level underneath him steady air,
        and striding
High there, how he rung upon the rein of a
    wimpling wing
In his ecstasy! then off, off forth on swing,
    As a skate's heel sweeps smooth on a bow-bend:
        the hurl and gliding
    Rebuffed the big wind. My heart in hiding
Stirred for a bird, the achieve of, the mastery of the
        thing!

Brute beauty and valour and act, oh, air, pride,
    plume here
        Buckle! AND the fire that breaks
        from thee then, a billion
Times told lovelier, more dangerous, O my chevalier!
    No wonder of it: sheer plod makes plough
        down sillion
Shine, and blue-bleak embers, ah my dear,
    Fall, gall themselves, and gash gold-vermilion.

Gerard Manley Hopkins

Easter Day

To him who is able to keep you from falling, and to bring you faultless and joyful before his glorious presence – to the only God our Saviour, through Jesus Christ our Lord, be glory, majesty, might, and authority, from all ages past, and now, and for ever and ever! Amen.

Jude, 24–25

AN ARUNDEL TOMB

Side by side, their faces blurred,
The earl and countess lie in stone,
Their proper habits vaguely shown
As jointed armour, stiffened pleat,
And that faint hint of the absurd –
The little dogs under their feet.

Such plainness of the pre-baroque
Hardly involves the eye, until
It meets his left-hand gauntlet, still
Clasped empty in the other; and
One sees, with a sharp tender shock,
His hand withdrawn, holding her hand.

They would not think to lie so long.
Such faithfulness in effigy
Was just a detail friends would see:
A sculptor's sweet commissioned grace
Thrown off in helping to prolong
The Latin names around the base.

They would not guess how early in
Their supine stationary voyage
The air would change to soundless damage,
Turn the old tenantry away;
How soon succeeding eyes begin
To look, not read. Rigidly they

Persisted, linked, through lengths and breadths
Of time. Snow fell, undated. Light
Each summer thronged the glass. A bright
Litter of birdcalls strewed the same
Bone-riddled ground. And up the paths
The endless altered people came,

Washing at their identity.
Now, helpless in the hollow of
An unarmorial age, a trough
Of smoke in slow suspended skeins
Above their scrap of history,
Only an attitude remains:

Time has transfigured them into
Untruth. The stone fidelity
They hardly meant has come to be
Their final blazon, and to prove
Our almost-instinct almost true:
What will survive of us is love.

Philip Larkin

Easter Day

I may be able to speak the languages of men and even of angels, but if I have no love, my speech is no more than a noisy gong or a clanging bell. I may have the gift of inspired preaching; I may have all knowledge and understand all secrets; I may have all the faith needed to move mountains – but if I have no love, I am nothing. I may give away everything I have, and even give up my body to be burnt – but if I have no love, this does me no good.

Love is patient and kind; it is not jealous or conceited or proud; love is not ill-mannered or selfish or irritable; love does not keep a record of wrongs; love is not happy with evil, but is happy with the truth. Love never gives up; and its faith, hope, and patience never fail.

Love is eternal. There are inspired messages, but they are temporary; there are gifts of speaking in strange tongues, but they will cease; there is knowledge, but it will pass. For our gifts of knowledge and of inspired messages are only partial; but when what is perfect comes, then what is partial will disappear.

When I was a child, my speech, feelings, and thinking were all those of a child; now that I am a man, I have no more use for childish ways. What we see now is like a dim image in a mirror; then we shall see face to face. What I know now is only partial; then it will be complete – as complete as God's knowledge of me.

Meanwhile these three remain: faith, hope, and love; and the greatest of these is love.

I Corinthians 13

Easter Day

Every book, every thought must have a love poem at its heart . . . do you remember how cross you were that the Litany said nothing about lovers? Death is a sort of love poem that can't go wrong.

Here's mine:

Love pirouettes
On a paradox
    where
nothing is all:
and to be fulfilled
(Everything you were meant to be)
is an emptying
into union
    with all love.

So, darling,
it is true:
I can love you
from my life's conglomeration
in this unexplained void
    where
my heart has lost its beating
in the Reality of meeting.

Anne Shells

Easter Day

A LETTER

Dear A,

. . . I meant to buy a wreath. But somehow couldn't face going into the shop and saying: 'No, I think tulips would be nicer'. So, I never went. Also there was the card. I didn't know what to write. 'Sympathy . . .? Deepest . . .?' Deepest what? I couldn't leave it blank and I couldn't write: THIS CAN'T BE THE END.

That's what came over me all the time: THIS CAN'T BE THE END.

It wasn't thinking back to remembered times, or because I felt – I'll keep him alive in my heart. It was more. It was much more. More than anything I knew about life up to the moment he died. It was the way his death brought a new dimension, and a hope. I knew there was more. I became sure. And somehow I couldn't send a wreath.

So I'm sitting down trying to apologise for this seeming neglect, darling. Because for you, God knows what it means – an emptiness? Is there any conviction through the crucifixion? Is there a prelude being played for the mysterious comprehension: THIS CAN'T BE THE END?

But surely I was wrong, a wreath is not finality but rather flowers promising a glory, a symbol of eternity. They, too, die to speak of this awareness of otherness. They witness the dispelling of gloom when one hears the thunderous awakening words:

THE RISING FROM THE TOMB.

And in this silent thrill, there is the excitement of an adventure ahead, suddenly, nothing to dread.

I regret not sending a wreath.

Anne Shells

Easter Day

Almighty God, who through thine only-begotten Son Jesus Christ hast overcome death, and opened unto us the gate of everlasting life: We humbly beseech thee, that as by thy special grace preventing us thou dost put into our minds good desires, so by thy continual help we may bring the same to good effect; through Jesus Christ our Lord, who liveth and reigneth with thee and the Holy Ghost, ever one God, world without end. Amen.

Collect for Easter Day,
Book of Common Prayer

Many, many years ago I was walking up through the bluebell woods at Bowringsleigh, near our home in south Devon. It was quite a steep path with beech trees on the left, and beyond the hedge on the right the view stretched away among up-and-down hills.

It was a spring evening, leaves at that lovely coming-out time, so beautiful that one must be exalted, but on this occasion something quite extra happened. There was the promise of an exceptional sunset, as the sun was now getting low in the sky. As I walked up the lane there was a moment of such sheer colour, I became unaware of myself having a body. I was aware only of being on the edge of the world (rather like the child in the fairy story of the Seven Ravens). I was waiting to leap off this edge into this glorious golden space. It is impossible to describe these sorts of moments. But it was 'out of this world'. When I became aware of myself again I knew I had seen death, that I had 'died', and it was utterly marvellous.

Anne Shells

Easter Day

LOVE UNFOLDING

And so I saw full surely that before ever God made us, he loved us. And this love was never quenched nor ever shall be. And in this love he has done all his works, and in this love he has made all things profitable to us, and in this love our life is everlasting. In our making we had beginning, but the love in which he made us was in him from without beginning, in which love we have our beginning.

Julian of Norwich

Trying to be cheerful – because I missed her badly – I went wearing a red hat to the memorial service of Daisy Knight Bruce. It was a mistake. I knew how wretched the last few weeks of her life had been, and there were only one or two others in that packed church who also knew this, so I reckoned we were gathered to give thanks for her life and rejoice. However, I felt conspicuous and managed to squash the hat into my handbag – or did I? After all these years I honestly don't remember whether I sat it out or bowed to convention. Churchgoers are always being faced with this problem, if not with hats any more, at least with a great many more important issues.

But then it is amazing how some church people behave in church; it's as though they leave their familiar selves outside the door and become most unnatural. Of course at most funerals the mourners have little confidence in the readings and prayers and are in any case in a state of distress, but the following conversation cannot be so unusual:

Many years and funerals since Daisy Knight Bruce's, I remember brave Mrs Grey. They had not long retired when Mr Grey died.

'So, Mr Grey has passed away.'

'Isn't it sad about Mr Grey.'

'Poor Mrs Grey . . .'

'Just after he was getting a little better.'

Oh, how they went on.

But Mrs Grey said:

'I'm glad for him, dear, you see he would never have gone on with his garden. He was a good man. I know he is better off where he is.'

That's what Mrs Grey said.

But the others went on.

'It's dreadful about Mr Grey, isn't it?'

They were STILL saying it after the funeral, after singing the hymns and hearing the statement:

Jesus said: THOUGH HE DIE, YET SHALL HE LIVE,
AND WHOEVER LIVES AND BELIEVES IN ME
SHALL NEVER DIE.

So when someone said to me: 'Oh, I do think it is so awfully sad about Mr Grey,' I could bear it no longer. I said: 'But you go to church every Sunday, don't you believe? Whatever do you think church is all about?'

And got the reply:

'Well, no-one has ever come back, have they?'

'NO-ONE HAS EVER COME BACK? JESUS CAME BACK!'

To which I got the answer:

'He was God.'

'But he was MAN!'

At that point it seemed better to mention the jumble sale, and let the Holy Spirit take over.

Anne Shells

Easter Day

Thanks be to you, O Christ, because you have broken for us the bonds of sin and brought us into fellowship with the Father.

Thanks be to you, O Christ, because you have triumphed over death, and opened to us the gates of eternal life.

Thanks be to you, O Christ, because where two or three are gathered together in your name, you are there among them.

Thanks be to you, O Christ, because you are alive for ever to intercede for us.

For these and all other benefits of your mighty resurrection, thanks be to you, O Christ.

Prayers for use at alternative services

Acknowledgements

The publishers gratefully acknowledge permission to reproduce the following copyright material:
Biblical extracts between pages 1–55: From the *New English Bible*, ©1970, by permission of Oxford and Cambridge University Presses.
Biblical extracts between pages 58–end: from *The Good News Bible*, ©American Bible Society 1976, by permission of the publishers, the Bible Societies/Collins.
1: 'You are a clown' by Annie Fratellini, from *The Times*, Jan. 16, 1984.
2: 'The true priest' by H. A. Williams, from *Someday I'll find you* (Mitchell Beazley).
3: 'It seems that enquiry' by Philip Toynbee, from *Part of a Journey* (Collins).

4: 'He had reached the point' by Laurens van der Post from *Yet Being Someone Other* (Chatto & Windus).
5: 'Love bade me welcome' by George Herbert.
6: 'By the grace of God' from *Rule for a New Brother*, published and ©1973 by Darton, Longman and Todd Ltd, London.
7: 'I am standing in a circle' by Rex Chapman, from *A Kind of Praying*, ©1970, SCM Press.
8: 'Oh, I hope I die' by Anne Shells, from an unpublished work, *Death our Brother*.
9: 'Lord, it is Holy Week' by Subir Biswas, from *Lord, Let Me Share*, ©Mrs Diana Biswas (Church Missionary Society).
10: 'Under a Dark Cloud' by George Appleton, from *Prayers from a Troubled Heart*, published and ©1983 by Darton, Longman and Todd Ltd, London.
11: 'O Lord Jesus Christ' adapted from a prayer of Launcelot Andrewes by David Silk, from *Prayers for Use at the Alternative Service* (Mowbrays); 'Lord Jesus Christ, who when about to institute' from the Royal Maundy Service ©Eyre and Spottiswoode.
12: 'Do not go gentle' by Dylan Thomas from *Collected Poems* (Dent).
14: 'An Evening Prayer' by Dag Hammarskjold from *Markings*, translated by W. H. Auden and Leif Sjoberg, by permission of Faber and Faber.
15: 'The Victorians destroyed Thackeray' by John Carey, from *The Sunday Times*, April 10, 1983.
16: 'In the midst of life' by Sidney G. Reeman, from *Beyond All Pain* by Cicely Saunders (SPCK).
17: 'Friday, 16th March' from the diary of Capt. Robert Falcon Scott.
19: 'I rest upon God' by John Austin Baker, from *Beyond All Pain*, by Cicely Saunders (SPCK).
20: 'Pilgrimages' by R. S. Thomas from *Frequencies*, by permission of the publishers, Macmillan, London and Basingstoke.
23: 'He wasn't alone' by Karol Wojtyla, from *Easter Vigil* (Hutchinson).

25: 'Suppose' by John Hencher, from *St Paul's, a Place to Dream* by John Hencher and Christopher Herbert (The Friends of St Paul's).
26: 'The Killing' by Edwin Muir, from *The Collected Poems of Edwin Muir*, by permission of Faber and Faber.
28: 'Death, be not proud' by John Donne.
29: 'God said to Adam' by Anne Shells, as above; 'Give rest, O Christ' from the Russian Orthodox Contakion of the Departed.
30: 'My earliest recollection' by Anne Shells, as above.
31: 'Tears' by Christopher Herbert, from *The Edge of Wonder* (CIO Publishing); 'And, of course, butterflies' by Anne Shells, as above.
32: Three prayers from *Student Prayer* (SCM Press, 1950).
33: 'Lord, they were very poor things' by Subir Biswas, as above.
34: 'Prayer of St Philip Howard' by St Philip Howard.
36: Three prayers by George Appleton from *Prayers from a Troubled Heart*, as above.
37: 'No one ever told me' by C. S. Lewis, from *A Grief Observed*, by permission of Faber and Faber.
39: 'The Late Wasp' by Edwin Muir, as above.
41: 'It is all grace' by John Austin Baker, from *Beyond All Pain*, as above.
42: 'After my funeral' by Anne Shells, as above.
44: 'We commend unto thee' by Bishop Launcelot Andrewes.
44: 'I never allowed myself' by Simone Weil, quoted by Anne Shells, as above.
44, 45: Prayers from *Student Prayer* (SCM Press).
46: 'Save us, O Lord' from the Service of Compline.
46: 'Lord, when I sleep' by Subir Biswas, as above.
47: 'Almighty and eternal God' from *A Christian's Prayer Book*, ed. Peter Coughlan, R. C. D. Jasper and T. Rodrigues OSB, by permission of Geoffrey Chapman, a division of Cassell Ltd.
48: 'The trees are singing', Sir Edward Elgar.
49: 'Now upon the bank' from *The Pilgrim's Progress*, by John Bunyan.